A Tribute to
THE YOUNG AT HEART

JUDY BLUME

By Jill C. Wheeler

Published by Abdo & Daughters, 4940 Viking Drive, Suite 622, Edina, Minnesota 55435.

Library bound edition distributed by Rockbottom Books, Pentagon Tower, P.O. Box 36036, Minneapolis, Minnesota 55435.

Printed in the United States.

Cover Photo credit: UPI/Bettmann
Interior Photo credits: UPI/Bettmann: p. 6, 10, 15, 27
Dell Publishing: p. 18

Edited by Julie Berg

Library of Congress Cataloging-in-Publication Data

Wheeler, Jill C., 1964-
Judy Blume / Jill C. Wheeler.
    p.   cm. -- (The young at heart)
Includes index.
Summary: Biography of the American writer who remembers so well what it was like to be young and who has written for young people for over twenty-five years.
ISBN 1-56239-490-8
1. Blume, Judy--Biography--Juvenile literature. 2. Novelists, American--20th century--Biography--Juvenile literature. 3. Children's stories--Authorship--Juvenile literature. [1. Blume, Judy. 2. Authors, American.] I. Title. II. Series: Tribute to the young at heart.
PS3552.L843Z98 1996
813'.52--dc20   95-41215
                                                                          CIP
                                                                           AC

Table of Contents

BUILDING *IGGIE'S HOUSE*

Judy Blume was nervous. She was about to meet publisher Richard Jackson and discuss a manuscript she had sent to him. She called the manuscript *Iggie's House*.

Magazines had published some of Judy's short stories. Yet no one had ever taken an interest in her novels. She wondered how the meeting would go. "My stomach was rolling, so I took something to calm it. Whatever I took dried up my mouth so that I could barely speak," she said.

Judy and Richard discussed the manuscript. It was about an African-American family who moves into an all-white neighborhood. Judy felt strongly about the subject. She had seen how rules separated African Americans and whites.

Richard liked the book idea. Still, he wanted to know more about the characters. Judy wrote down his questions and suggestions. She agreed to make some changes and return the manuscript.

Judy spent a month revising the manuscript. She sent it back to Richard and waited eagerly. At last, Richard called her. His company would publish the book. The news thrilled Judy. Even before *Iggie's House* was in bookstores, Judy was at work on another novel.

Judy's love of writing has not changed. In 25 years, she has written more than 20 books for young people. Many have won awards. Some were made into movies.

Her many fans are most important to her. "I have a wonderful, intimate relationship with kids," she said. "It's rare and lovely. They feel that they know me and that I know them." Recalling what it's like to be a child is the key to her success. She remembers what it's like to have so many unanswered questions.

Author Judy Blume, 1978.

STORIES AND DREAMS

Young Judy Sussman filled her life with stories. She made up stories about her dolls. She listened to scary stories on the radio. She saw stories in what her family did each day. She also heard stories about something called "the war."

Judy was born on February 12, 1938, in Elizabeth, New Jersey. She was barely four years old when the United States entered World War II. Her father, Rudolph, was an air-raid warden. He had to prepare the town for an enemy attack. Luckily, it never came.

After the war, life returned to normal for the Sussmans. Rudolph worked as a dentist. Judy and her big brother, David, went to school and played. Judy continued to make up stories. She liked to pretend she was a ballerina in the movies. She wanted to be a movie star someday.

Judy also loved to read. She often went to the library with her mother. "I not only liked the pictures and the stories, but also the feel and the smell of the books," she remembered. "Books opened up a whole new world to me. Through them, I discovered new ideas, traveled to new places, and met new people. Books helped me learn to understand other people and they taught me a lot about myself."

Judy's happy childhood took a sad turn when she was ten years old. First, her grandmother died. Then her aunt passed away. Death was scary and puzzling for Judy. She had many questions. What was it like to die? What was it like to become a grown woman? She tried to find books that answered her questions. None of them did.

When she was in third grade, Judy's family had another scary experience. Her brother became very sick. The doctors said he needed to live someplace warmer. New Jersey was not warm in the fall and winter. Judy's family decided to move to Miami Beach, Florida, for the winter. Her brother would get better there.

Judy was not happy to leave home. Her father had to stay in New Jersey to work. Judy and her father were very close. She called him "Doey-bird." She knew she would miss him terribly. He promised to visit the family often.

NEW PLACES, NEW FACES

The train ride to Florida took a day and a half. During the trip, the conductor said all African-American people had to go to the back of the train. Judy asked her mother why.

Her mother explained that in the South, African Americans and whites didn't ride together. People called this segregation. Judy didn't think that was fair. She never forgot about it.

Judy grew to love Miami Beach. She and her family spent two winters there while her brother healed. Judy made many new friends and took ballet lessons with

Miami Beach, Florida, in the 1950s where Judy Blume
spent her childhood winters.

them. She entered a contest to win a pair of ballet shoes worn by a famous dancer. Later, Judy wrote about that contest in her book *Starring Sally J. Freedman As Herself*.

At the beach, Judy tried to learn to swim, but she had trouble putting her head under water. She finally succeeded when she went to summer camp in Connecticut. When she was fifteen, she changed camps. While she was there, her other grandmother died. Judy never forgot how that felt. She wrote about it in her book *Forever*.

Judy was very sad to lose her grandmother. But she could not talk about it with her parents. She didn't want to tell them how the sad news had ruined her fun at camp. She thought they would be disappointed. More and more, she hid her feelings. She kept wishing for someone to talk to.

In high school, Judy kept busy. She worked on the school newspaper. She performed with the school's dance troupe. She and her friends dreamed of being famous actresses. They also attended many parties—with boys. Judy enjoyed meeting boys. After graduation she decided to attend Boston College because a friend had told her that's where the boys were.

Judy didn't stay long at Boston College. She became sick shortly after she arrived, and missed the first semester. After that, she attended New York University. When she was a sophomore, she met John Blume at a party. He was a law student.

John and Judy spent much time together. Finally, John asked Judy to marry him. Shortly before the wedding, Judy's father died. His death hurt Judy deeply. She had loved her father more than anyone. Yet Judy's religion said a couple must not cancel their wedding once they've set a date. Judy and John were married on August 15, 1959.

WIFE AND MOTHER

Judy attended college after her marriage and graduated in 1960. In February 1961, she gave birth to a girl. Judy and John named her Randy. Judy had planned to teach school after she graduated. Now, she put her career on hold to stay with her baby. Two years later, her son Larry was born.

Judy was twenty-five years old. She had a husband, two children and a house. Most people thought her life was perfect. Judy felt something was missing. But she couldn't express her feelings to anyone.

"I don't think any of us at that time ever really admitted what we were feeling," she said. "Or what life was like or what our hopes and dreams were." Judy tried to fill the empty space in her life. She wrote songs. She made banners for children. Then she tried writing children's books.

She sent her stories to publishers. They came back rejected. At first, it was hard to accept the rejections. Few people understood why she wanted to write. "When I started to write, there were a lot of people who were genuinely resentful," she said. "The lack of support was jarring." Gradually, Judy learned to deal with the rejections.

One day, she received a brochure in the mail for a class at New York University called "Writing for Children and Teenagers." She enrolled in the class. She enjoyed being back in school. The class was so helpful she took it twice. Her instructor believed in her work. "She would write me little notes telling me I would get published one day," Judy remembered.

Judy Blume is known and loved by millions of readers for her funny,
honest, always believable stories.

PUBLISHED!

Judy soon sold two short stories to magazines. It had taken more than two years, but now she was a published author. Shortly after that, she sold a short book called *The One In The Middle is the Green Kangaroo*. Judy's family celebrated when the book was published. The local newspaper ran a story about it.

John was glad his wife had published her book. Yet he thought she should be making more money for her hard work. Judy didn't care about the money. She just loved to write.

Judy wrote *Iggie's House* as a homework assignment for her writing class. The book began her longtime relationship with her editor, Richard Jackson.

Even as she revised *Iggie's House* for Richard, Judy wanted to write a book about what was important to her as a young girl. When Judy was young, she had long talks with God about everything. She even told

God she was the last of her friends to get her period. Judy wrote the book in just six weeks.

"I just let go and wrote what I wanted to write," she said. "I told the truth about what I felt." The book was titled *Are You There God? It's Me, Margaret.*

Judy was nervous about the book reviews. The critics had not liked her first two books, which they called too simple. Judy thought this book would be different. It was the first book she'd written from her heart.

She was right. Critics loved *Margaret.* The book won four awards. The *New York Times Book Review* called *Margaret* one of the best books for children in 1970. Judy was very happy. For the first time in her life, she felt she was a real author. She said, "That was the first I felt, 'I really can do this! These people are taking me seriously! It's not just pretend.'"

The cover of the Judy Blume book *Are You There God? It's Me, Margaret.*

Despite the good reviews, some people didn't want anyone to read *Margaret,* including the librarian at her children's school. She said they didn't allow any books that discussed menstruation. Other libraries banned the book, too.

That didn't stop children from reading it. Many children began writing letters to Judy. They told her they loved her books. They told her they felt like she knew what they were feeling. Judy was happy to hear they liked her books. She kept writing more and more.

WRITING THROUGH TOUGH TIMES

In 1971, Judy wrote *Then Again, Maybe I Won't.* The book is about a boy's questions while growing up. She also wrote *Freckle Juice*, a funny story about a boy who thinks he has too many freckles. *Tales of a Fourth Grade Nothing* and *Otherwise Known as Sheila the Great* came out in 1972. *Tales* continues to be one of

Judy's most popular books. It's about a boy, Peter Hatcher, and the younger brother who makes his life difficult. Like *Margaret*, it won many awards.

Judy enjoyed writing funny books. But she wrote serious ones, too. *It's Not the End of the World* is about a girl trying to accept her parents' divorce. *Deenie* is about a girl who learns she has scoliosis. Scoliosis is a disease where a person's spine becomes curved. In *Blubber*, Judy wrote about being overweight and having classmates tease you.

Those books prepared Judy for the one she would write next. Her daughter, Randy, asked her to write a realistic teenage love story. The result was *Forever*, about a young woman's first love. Many adults didn't like the book's realism. They thought Judy Blume had gone too far. But Judy's young readers loved it.

Meanwhile, Judy was having her own problems. Her sixteen-year marriage to John Blume was breaking up. She felt she had changed too much since she married him. "I don't think my choice of John was wrong at the time," she said. "It reflected everything I knew of life."

Judy and her children moved to Princeton, New Jersey. Shortly after that, she met Tom Kitchens. They became good friends. Then, Tom moved to London. Judy and her children followed him, and lived there for six months. Soon Judy and Tom got married. The whole family returned to the United States to live in New Mexico.

Unfortunately, Judy's second marriage was an unhappy one. She admitted she married Tom too quickly. "We didn't know each other. I cried for four years, but I learned a lot," she said. Judy and Tom worked on their marriage for three years, but they were unsuccessful. They divorced in 1979. Judy remained in New Mexico. "I loved the white and the sunshine," she said. "I loved the bright colors."

While suffering the pain of another divorce, she kept writing. In 1977 she wrote *Starring Sally J. Freedman as Herself*. The book used many true stories from Judy's childhood. She also wrote a novel for adults called *Wifey*.

That worried her young readers. What if she stopped writing for them? She erased their worries in 1980. *Superfudge* came out with more stories about Peter Hatcher and his siblings. *Superfudge* sold more copies than any of her other books. Judy was back.

RELATING TO HER READERS

By 1995, Judy had written more than 20 books for children, young adults and adults. People have criticized some of her books. Yet most people praise her work. Book reviewers say her books are written so readers can relate to what's happening.

Judy is successful because she remembers so well what it was like to be young.

"I have a capacity for total recall," she said. "That's my talent, if there's a talent involved. I have this gift, this memory, so it's easy to project myself back to certain stages in my life. And I write about what I know is true of kids going through those same stages."

Judy uses a first-person narrative writing style to make her books lively. First-person is when the person telling the story refers to himself or herself as "I." This makes her books read like diaries or journals.

One reviewer had another opinion. "Judy Blume is not the most popular author alive today just because she looks like a kid," he said. "She is popular because what she writes about and how she writes it make her characters and their actions more real than anything anyone else writes."

Judy also feels it's important that young people realize they can achieve their dreams. She didn't have many choices when she was young.

"I went to college to be a teacher because I was influenced by my mother's practical wishes for me," she said. "I knew my goal in college was to meet a man and get married. My mother said to get a degree in education in case I ever had to work, but I wasn't really thinking. I was very busy wanting to get married and have babies and play grown-up."

Judy receives about 2,000 fan letters a month. In 1986, she put some in a book titled *Letters to Judy: What Your Kids Wish They Could Tell You*.

"The impression I get, from letter after letter, is that a great many kids don't communicate with their parents," she said. "They feel alone in the world. Sometimes, reading books that deal with other kids who feel the same things makes them feel less alone."

Judy hopes both parents and young people read *Letters to Judy* so they can learn to talk together. She donates the book royalties to the KIDS Fund, which she started in 1981. The fund gives money to nonprofit organizations that encourage young people to talk to their parents.

ANSWERING THE CRITICS

Judy wants young people to talk to their parents about the subjects that interest them, such as sex, religion and how their bodies change as they grow up. Judy says these topics interested her as a child. That's why she writes about them now. Yet writing about them has made her controversial.

"I write about sexuality because it was uppermost in my mind when I was a kid," she said. "My father delivered these little lectures to me on how babies are made. But questions about what I was feeling, and how my body could feel, I never asked my parents."

Judy believes that discussion is the best way to address controversial questions. She discusses these questions in her books, so it makes her angry when people want to ban them. "The way to instill values in children is to talk about difficult issues," she said. "Not to restrict their access to books that may help them deal with their problems and concerns."

Judy is careful not to judge young people and tell them what to do. Instead, she shows them what her characters learn along the way. She wishes she had these books when she was young.

"I wrote these books a long time ago when there wasn't anything near the censorship that there is now," she added. "I wasn't aware at the time that I was writing anything controversial. I just know what these books would have meant to me when I was a kid."

Today's readers *do* know what Judy's books mean. Millions of young people have bought her books and continue to do so. Her book *Forever* was made into a movie. Artists made an animated feature based on her *Freckle Juice* book. Soon her "Fudge" characters will be a part of a television show.

Judy Blume, children's book author.

A FIFTY-YEAR-OLD KID

Even though she's in her 50s, Blume said she feels like she's "12 on the inside."

While writing *Fudge-a-Mania*, she said she "fantasized about someday being a grandma who catches a fly ball while playing third base."

In June 1987, Judy married writer George Cooper. The two live in New York City. On their honeymoon, Judy spoke to a group of school children.

Judy plans to write and make more magic for her many readers. "Some books you never forget," she said. "Some characters become your friends for life."

She added that the worst thing for a writer "is when you don't have a book or two in mind. You're always worried that you'll never have another idea." Fortunately for her fans, that hasn't happened yet.

GLOSSARY

Banned— when a booked is censored.

Censorship — when people try to stop other people from reading or listening to certain things.

Character — a person in a novel or play.

Controversial — something people don't agree about.

First-Person Narrative — a style of writing where the person telling the story refers to himself or herself as "I."

Jarring — upsetting.

Manuscript — the text of a book or story before it is published.

Menstruation — the monthly discharge of blood that begins at puberty for girls.

Novel — a long story.

Period — another word for menstruation.

Resentful — when people are bothered by something.

Scoliosis — a disease where a person's spine develops a curve.

Segregation — separating people based on the color of their skin.

Index